FAMILY DRAMA

Attractive Parcel

BEATRICE NDUDIM GOLDSON-NWALOZIE

PAPERBACK: 978-1-950540-88-4
EBOOK: 978-1-950540-89-1

Ordering Information:

For orders and inquiries, please contact:
1-888-375-9818
www.toplinkpublishing.com
bookorder@toplinkpublishing.com

Printed in the United States of America

CONTENTS

DEDICATION

This book "FAMILY DRAMA" is dedicated to Jehovah, "The Almighty, All-sufficient God who gave me the grace, strength, knowledge, wisdom, exciting great and healthy life to start and complete this work at His own time. All glory, honor, power, dominion, excellence, majesty be ascribed unto Him alone. Amen.

ACKNOWLEDGEMENT

I cannot express enough thanks to Professor Pai Obanya former UNESCO Director, Dakar, Senegal, for his continued support and encouragement to start and complete this book.

My special thanks goes to my wonderful friends and colleagues for their good advice in making the production of this book a success: Mrs. Obiageri Akajelu of the Ministry of Foreign Affairs, Nigeria. Mrs. Ngozi Obinani, former Deputy Director, Federal Ministry of Education, Abuja. Dr. Mrs.Patience Ozor, Alvan Ikoku College of Education, Owerri, Imo State. Dr. Mrs. Bridget Ikegwuru, Federal Government College, Port-Harcourt, Rivers State. Mrs. Constance M. Kalu Nwoke, Chief Scientific Officer, State Ministry of Health, Umuahia, Abia State. Barr. Mrs. Pearl Ebiringa, Imo State University, Owerri. Mrs. Claris Ujam, Deputy Director, Federal Ministry of Education, Abuja. Dr. Mrs. Chidi Nwosu, Imo State University, Owerri. Mr. and Mrs. Raymond Okoroji of MTA, New York. I appreciate all your efforts and wonderful advice. Thank you.

My completion of this book could not have been accomplished without the support of my beloved children: Chichi –Daughter-Florida, Akachi – Son- Boston, and Chubby –Son-Georgia who were there for me, patiently and passionately sharing my hopes and dreams, defeats and despairs, triumphs and elations and all through the period of writing this book. Thank you sweethearts may the Almighty God bless you all.

This page cannot be completed without my special thanks to the UNESCO Library, Brenda, Dakar, Senegal for providing me with most of the books used and the Public Library, Eastchester, E. Gun Hill road, Bronx, New York, for assisting me with the very important books that were relevant and useful to me. My heartfelt thanks.

PREFACE

This book "Family Drama" was started in 1999 in Dakar, Senegal, a West African country due to an unpleasant experience in my family.

Once a peaceful family became unstable as the sea. I was advised by good friends to start writing a book on my experience to benefit numerous ladies and families with similar experience.

There were lots of hitches on the way all these while which prevented the publishing of this book in 2009 when it was ready, such as virus attack on my computer.

I am grateful to God, finally, it's here.

INTRODUCTION

FAMILY STRUCTURE

Family life is most precious. It is the natural environment for the growth and wellbeing of all family members particularly children. Love, mutual respect, gender equality, solid inter-generational links, and supportive emotional bonding should be its hallmarks.

From a sociological viewpoint, households or families are traditional institutions for reproduction and child rearing. One's family is a source of emotional support and a vehicle for socialization for its members. On the other hand, family is a unit of economic production in a traditional agrarian setting. Production is carried out in the home or on the land adjacent to it and a household members, often including children, contribute to a productive activities.

Household or family members rely on and contribute to those functions in varying ways and degrees over the course of their lives. At the same time, the functions of individual household members are often determined by family characteristics-sizes, type or structure- since these characteristics affect the relationships and obligations of the members.

Conventional typologies usually divide families into nuclear and extended families. A nuclear family consists of a married couple and their unmarried children or a single parent and unmarried children, whereas an extended family comprises, in addition to a nuclear family unit a broader set of relations and sometimes unrelated individuals. Families can be extended both vertically and horizontally, for instance, a three- generation family made up to an elder conjugal couple, with their son and his wife and grand –children, is a well-known variety of extended family. Also, a horizontally extended family, which includes two or more brothers and their wives and children, is often referred to as a joint family. The family pattern of traditional Hindu society in India is an example of this (Adams, 1986)., but a part of us dies without an intimate connection.

We are created to love and be loved, and there is no greater opportunity for this love than in marriage. We are called to become one with another so that we can touch each other's deepest needs: the need for security-knowing that we are loved-and the need for significance-knowing that we are valued. So why marriage disintegration? Lack of love, communication, immigration? In other to be successful in marriage, you have to be solid, responsible and whole. That means you have to love yourself, delight in the unique creation of you, and appreciate the unique creation reflected in others. You have to be able to love yourself before you can love anyone else, study yourself and your purpose in life-yet marriage will not tolerate selfishness.

We all desperately long for a happy relationship. We were born into relationships, helpless and vulnerable, and had it not been relationships, we would have perished. Not much has changed except that we can physically survive

The wish of couples to create stable environments for themselves and their children runs strong and deep. Present difficulties encountered in family life are often a reflection of far-reaching economic, social and demographic changes. During certain critical years, almost all parents need support in their task of providing care and education for their children. Even more so, vulnerable families- single-parent families without shelter or income, immigrant families, destabilized families, the community, and society at large.

The aim of social support is not to take away parental functions or to make families passive recipients of social care. Having children creates responsibility and will normally motivate parent to carry out their biological, psychological, economical and education functions: to impart care and protection; often love and healthy family relationship; provide shelter and material welfare; promote play and learning. Societies will do well, however to support responsible attitudes to parenthood by educating adolescents and young adults in parenting skills and providing support systems for parents in their child-rearing tasks.

The international year of the family in 1994 provides the occasion for reflection on the family, as the "smallest democracy at the heart of society", the phenomenon of the absent father is widespread. His reduced participation in parenting is sometimes the result of external causes such as migration for work, but more often it is the result of deep -seated cultural attitudes and gender stereotyping. Even in what should be fairly ideal circumstances, father often spend little time with their children. Yet, research suggests that many mothers are, as a result, over worked, and that boys, in particular, suffer from paternal absence. In addition, non-support by father undermines the economic base of a growing number of women-headed families.

Families of migrants at the place of origin must adjust not only to the permanent or temporary absence of family members, but also to the influences of the newly acquired money, goods, ideas, attitudes, behavior and innovations transmitted back to them by the mover. The adjustment to these active impacts that families must make depend upon which family members move, the length of the absence, and the socio-cultural system at the place of origin.

The nuclear family is often more economically viable than the extended group, which has become less frequent in the majority of cities. Rural-to- urban migration frequently reinforces this pattern. Census data for example shows that 80% of migrants to Indian cities settle in nuclear families rather than the traditional joint family system.

In 1992 rewrite Marriage and Recession annual report, UK marriage Guidance Group, stated that unemployment, redundancy, home repossessions, and mounting debts have a devastating effect on family life of the people.

African family in particular, is under great pressure. Average per-capita income fell by a quarter in the 1990s, between 1979 and 1985 the number of Africans living below the poverty line increased by almost two-thirds. Per capital incomes have also decreased in Latin America and parts of Asia, swamping improvements in other areas such as China. But in Africa, environmental degradation, increasing population, and food insecurity have combined to undermine the family's ability to cope in a situation made worst by national debt and world recession.

Many important events take place in the home. It is here that family members receive shelter and sustenance. Home is possibly the most important place in all our lives; it is where we belong and feel secured.

Some family members can never leave home or establish an independent life. This may be due to illness or disability; it may be due to infirmity in old age.

In the absence of wider support, the family provides safety for those unable to care for themselves. Indeed, the family is the most important welfare institution in the world. As the mother's body provides the first protection to the developing child, so the family provides a supportive boundary around its members a 'heaven in a heartless world'.

In most societies, it is mothers who provide the caring for infants, because they spend considerable amount of time together, mothers and children get to know each other well and develop close emotionally. These ties are a powerful source of happiness and identity for all. Family relations are emotionally affected, love and affection, anger and aggression among others, all find expression in families. Emotional expression is a deeply important part of children's development, and it is encouraged through play. Often it is during their leisure time that family members are most intimate with one another. Indeed providing recreation is a role of the family.

Evidence clearly shows that a child who is neglected physically, mentally, or emotionally will suffer disadvantages which may last a life time. The family is still regarded as the best environment for a young child's nurture and upbringing, even in disadvantaged circumstances. In a troubled family, the reverse is the case, but on the whole, parents try to avoid divided families. The thought of losing custody or worst still contact with the child is phobic. More so, vulnerable families-single-parent families, families without shelter or income, immigrant families, destabilized families, or families with special needs, need the support of the extended family, the community, and society at large.

CHAPTER 1

COURTSHIP AND DATING GAME

Courtship is the traditional dating period before engagement and Marriage (or long term commitment if marriage is not allowed). It is an alternative to arranged marriages in which the couple or group does not meet before the wedding…One way courtship varies is in the duration; courting can take days or years.

The institution of marriage is likely to continue but some previous patters of marriage will become outdated as new patterns emerge. Cohabitation contributes to the phenomenon of people getting married for the first time at a later age than was typical in earlier generations (Glezer, 1991). Furthermore, marriage will continue to be delayed as more people place education and career ahead of 'settling down'.

Courtship varies both by time period and by region of the world. One way courtship varies in the duration, courting can take days or years. In the United Kingdom, a poll of 3,000 engaged or married couples suggested an average between first meeting and engagement of 2 years and 11 months. (Lumen Learning, Courses)

Dating is a casual time of fun and getting acquainted. For this reason, family has always encouraged group dates, several couples going to a ball game. Dating has nothing in view but simple enjoyment and getting acquainted with members of the opposite sex. In a sense dates are fact finding mission. Going steady is a prelude to engagement, it is actually courtship. Dating can naturally lead to courtship. This will take place when the field is narrowed and considerable fact finding has taken place. It has often been said every date is a potential mate. This is true, the dating process should have been the objective of screening out the characters you detested from each other.

MARRIAGE

Marriage, also called matrimony or wedlock, is a socially or ritually recognized union between spouses that establishes rights and obligations between those spouses, as well as between them and any resulting biological or adopted children and affinity (In-laws and other family through marriage). The definition of marriage varies around the world not only between cultures and between religions, but also throughout the history of any given culture and religion, evolving to both expand and constrict in who and what is encompassed, but typically it is principally an institution in which interpersonal relationships, usually sexual., are acknowledged or sanctioned. In some cultures, marriage is recommended or considered to be compulsory before pursuing any sexual activity. When defining broadly, marriage is considered a cultural universal. A marriage ceremony is known a Wedding.

Individuals may marry for several reasons, including legal, social, emotional, spiritual, financial, and religious purposes. Whom they marry may be influenced by socially determined rules. Parental choice and individual desire. In some areas of the world, arrange marriage, child marriage, polygamy, and sometimes forced marriage, may be practiced as a cultural tradition. Conversely, such practices may be outlawed and penalized in parts of the world out of concerns of the infringement of women's rights, or the infringement of children's rights (both female and male children), and because of international law. Around the world, primarily in developed democracies, there has been a general trend towards ensuring equal rights within marriage for women and legally recognizing the marriages of interfaith, interracial, and same-sex couples. These trends coincide with the broader human rights movement.

Marriage can be recognized by a state, an organization, a religious authority, a tribal group, a local community, or peers. It is often viewed as a contract. When a marriage is performed and carried out by a government institution in accordance with the marriage laws of the jurisdiction, without religious content, it is a civil marriage. Civil marriage recognizes and creates the rights and obligations intrinsic to matrimony before the state. When a marriage is performed with religious content under the auspices of a religious institution it is a religious marriage. Religious marriage recognizes and creates the rights and obligations intrinsic to matrimony before that religion. Religious marriage is known variously as sacramental marriage in Catholicism, nikah in Islam, nissuin in Judaism, and various other names in other faith traditions, each with their own constraints as to what constitutes, and who can enter into, a valid religious marriage.

Some countries do not recognize locally performed religious marriage on its own, and require a separate civil marriage for official purposes. Conversely, civil marriage does not exist in some countries governed by a religious legal system, such as Saudi Arabia, where marriages contracted abroad might not be recognized if they were contracted contrary to Saudi interpretations of Islamic religious law. In countries governed by a mixed secular-religious legal system, such as in Lebanon and Israel, locally performed civil marriage also does not exist within the country, preventing interfaith and various other marriages contradicting religious laws from being entered into in the country, however, civil marriages performed abroad are recognized by the state even if they conflict with religious laws (in the case of recognition of marriage in Israel, this includes recognition of not only interfaith civil marriages performed abroad, but also overseas same-sex civil marriages).

The act of marriage usually creates normative or legal obligations between the individuals involved, and any offspring they may produce or adopt. In terms of legal recognition, most sovereign states and other jurisdictions limit marriage to opposite-sex couples and a diminishing number of these permit polygyny, child marriages, and forced marriages. In modern times, a growing number of countries, primarily developed democracies, have lifted bans on and have established legal recognition for the marriages of interfaith, interracial, and same-sex couples. Some cultures allow the dissolution of marriage through divorce or annulment. In some areas, child marriages and polygamy may occur in spite of national laws against the practice.

Since the late twentieth century, major social changes in Western countries have led to changes in the demographics of marriage, with the age of first marriage increasing, fewer people marrying, and more couples choosing to cohabit rather than marry. For example, the number of marriages in Europe decreased by 30% from 1975 to 2005.

Historically, in most cultures, married women had very few rights of their own, being considered, along with the family's children, the property of the husband; as such, they could not own or inherit property, or represent themselves legally (see for example coverture). In Europe, the United States, and other places in the developed world, beginning in the late 19th century and lasting through the 21st century, marriage has undergone gradual legal changes, aimed at improving the rights of the wife. These changes included giving wives legal identities of their own, abolishing the right of husbands to physically discipline their wives, giving wives property rights, liberalizing divorce laws, providing wives with reproductive rights of their own, and requiring a wife's consent when sexual relations occur. These changes have occurred primarily in Western countries. In the 21st century, there continue to be controversies regarding the legal status of married women, legal acceptance of or leniency towards violence within marriage (especially sexual violence), traditional marriage customs such as dowry and bride price, forced marriage, marriageable age, and criminalization of consensual behaviors such as premarital and sex outside marriage(Wikipedia)

FAMILY AND RESPONSIBILITIES

Having children creates responsibility and will normally motivate parents to carry out their biological, psychological, economic and educational functions: to impart care and protection; offer love and healthy family relationships; provide shelter and material welfare; and promote play and learning.

Children, combined with the bitterness and anger of a failed relationship, make separation and divorce one of the most terrible experiences endured by adults. For most divorce is a last resort, not simply to end a nightmare, but sometimes for survival.

Broken families can result from separation due to illness, divorce or other issues. The break-up of a family has many negative impacts on the children. The children are more likely to act out against siblings, biological parents or stepparents. Children also develop emotional issues, such as anger, resentment, loneliness and depression, due to the change in the family unit. Children involved in broken families are also more likely to engage in early sexual activities.

With growing economic indecency of women in many regions, it is possible for them to consider raising their children alone. Divorce is also common in areas of high unemployment, rapid urbanization, and social change. Divorce does not indicate a loss of belief in marriage-many divorces remarry- but second and third marriages have even higher incidences of breakdown.

However, marital breakdown is often followed by moving to a new area, changing jobs, and starting a new family. These developments are often used as a pretext for losing touch with children from a previous marriage.

We should all recognize that successful family life is neither enforced dependency, nor isolated individualism, but interdependence within families, this, implies a relationship between equals- gender and generation. Within communities, social institutions should support families enough to empower them, but not trap them in dependency.

Like everything else in nature, the family is subject to continuous change. That which is static in nature, dies. Children grow up, parents grow old, and other children are born. We know about the endless cycle of life, and it is the glory of the family that it is the logical team to make the best and face the worse of what this world has to offer. It is a practical example of the necessary interdependence of the human race, able, ideally, to counter most vicissitudes and even to accept generalizations and platitudes with that necessary pinch of salt.

THE CONCEPT OF FAMILIES

In the United States the concepts of family has changed during the past two generations. During the latter half of 20th century in the United States , the proportion of married couples with children shrank- such families made up only 24 percent of all households in 2000(Fields and Casper 2001). The idea of family has come to signify many familiar arrangements, including blended families, divorced single mothers or fathers with children, never married women with children, cohabiting heterosexual partners, and gay or lesbian families (Bianchi and Casper, 2000).

The increase in single-mother families, which typically have greater per-person expenses and less earning power, may help to explain why, in the general prosperity of the last half of the 2oth century, the percentage of children living in the poorest families almost doubled, rising from 15 to 28 percent (Bianchi and Casper 2000).

Bengtson (2001) asserts that relationships involving three or more generations increasingly are becoming important to individuals and families, that these relationships increasingly are diverse in structure and functions, and that for many Americans, multi-generational bonds are important ties for well-being and support over the course of their lives.

FAMILY AS AN ECOSYSTEM

Substance abuse impairs physical and mental health, and it strains and taxes the agencies that promote physical and mental health. In families with substance abuse, family members often are connected not just to each other but also to any of a number of government agencies, such as social services, criminal justice, or child protective services. The economic toll includes a huge drain on individuals 'employability and other elements of productivity. The social and economic costs are felt in many workplaces and homes.

The ecological perspective on substance abuse views people as nested in various systems. Individual are nested in families; families are nested in communities. Kaufman (1999) identifies members of the ecosystem of an individual with a substance abuse problem as family, peers (those in recovery as well as those still using), treatment providers, non-family support sources, the workplace, and legal system.

A young couple married when they were 25 and 20 years old. One spouse developed alcoholism during the first 7 years of their marriage. The couple's life increasingly became chaotic and painful for another 7 years, when finally ,at age 30 of the man, the substance abusing partner entered treatment after messing up the financial, social, emotional life of the marriage. He was in treatment over the course of 18 months, attained a solid degree of sobriety. Suddenly, lack of communication and difficulties with intimacy came to the fore for the non-substance abusing lady, who now often feels sad and hopeless about the marital relationship. The non- substance abusing spouse finds out that after 18 months of the partners 'sobriety, he still does not want to make plans for another child.

Almost all young couples encounter communication and intimacy issues during the first decade of their relationship. In an alcoholic marriage or relationship, such issues are regularly pushed into the background as guilt, blame, and control, issues are exacerbated by the nature of addictive disease and its effects on both the relationship and the family thereby having a real family drama.

CHAPTER 2

EXCITEMENT IN MARRIAGE

Family is a universal phenomenon. The Family is the oldest, most fundamental, and most enduring of all human institutions. It is the cornerstone of society and our personal lives. It is the source of the new generation, of population growth or control, and of primary child care. It meets the basic human needs of food and shelter, care for elderly and disabled people, creates wealth and provides large, unrecognized economic services.

Family means socialization, education and transmitter of culture, tradition and skills. The family can profoundly influence our human potential and happiness by the care it offers in our youth. All our lives we turned to it for love and shared values, for support in good times or bad, and as a reference point that gives meaning to our experience.

We learn from family contact throughout our lives: each important experience, such as marriage, having children or retiring, brings new patterns of behavior with it. Learning is most intense during infancy and childhood. The mother is normally the principal teacher of the very young child, at least until weaning. But as the infant's horizons expand, so other people begin to have growing influence. Older siblings, especially sisters, are important because often they care for the young child. Marriage is a socially recognized union of a man and woman as husband and wife which was instituted by God. It legitimizes sexual access and brings procreation which ensures the continuity of lineage.

THE NORMAL LIFE

It has been so good getting married and everything falling in place as expected. Being matured to marry, meeting loved one, dating, getting to meet with each other's family members and formalizing the marriage as the culture would have it. Quite an interesting and exciting process where all relations that has helped in your growing up are brought into the picture. When the rites performance are completed, couples relax and form their nuclear family.

As little your finance might be as young beginners, you wouldn't mind as long as you live together, you begin to manage, face your responsibilities and to make ends meet

Much of human activity is directed towards the realization of personal aims and ambitions, especially in terms of marriage, the maintenance of the home and the establishment of a family. It would seem a much more valid interpretation that man works to eat and to provide a living for his dependents and that much of his youthful efforts is devoted to acquiring such defendants.

The family evolves, for thousands of years it has adapted to a constantly changing world. Families vary so much within regions and among cultures. There is no simple view of the family: no universal definition. Most of us assume we know exactly what family is. We might say that it is a household, a group of people who live together under the same roof and who are related. A family is not always tied to one place and to one time. A family may split between households. The family exerts a powerful influence over its members, requiring them to respect and preserve the blood line, conserve family tradition and class, and to protect the family's reputation. Our ancestry has considerable bearing on our expectations in life. The ability of the family to control destiny stretches across the generations: some believe its stems from the dead. Ancestral cults are important in many societies. We all are fascinated with our origins-our 'Roots'. Some people travel halfway across the world, at great expense, to trace ancestors and draw up a family tree.

Economic, technological and social developments are having a powerful impact on families. A growing number of couples do not have children: perhaps as many as a third of families have only one parent, (and some center on the partnership of two adults of the same sex)

Exhibiting caring values within the family is the surest way to protect and promote the rights and welfare of individual members. The health and wellbeing of young children, for example, is dramatically improved by teaching parents about birth spacing, hygiene, good nutrition and safety within the home. Informed parents can help prevent disability, alcohol and drug addiction, violence and neglect. They can also cater for the special needs of disabled members by learning basic rehabilitation techniques.

Since women are primarily responsible for child rearing and domestic matters, most family polices and information on family welfare is targeted at them. But programs to involve men in family life are badly needed, if only to ensure the fair distribution of responsibly.

DATING GAME

COMPANIONSHIP

This is to avoid loneliness because there are lots of psych-social problems and emotional disturbances that can emanate from a matured man or woman that is staying alone. Everybody needs a friend, a partner, someone to lean on, to talk to, a person that can be depended upon in times of need, a trusted person. This in itself is the real purpose of marriage. Husband and wife should be true friends that manifest loyalty and faithfulness to the last among themselves.

A partner that can be leaned on, dependable, trust for this is the purpose of marriage. This partnership is meant to last for a life time. The imperatives are that you are to leave your original family where you belong to join with the family of your spouse (partner). For this great miracle to take place, there must be a pre-requisite which is' LOVE' that creates attraction amongst you, but this love must be a genuine one in order to empower you to take this giant step of life. Love is a powerful emotion felt for another person manifesting itself in deep affection, it attracts, magnetizes and it involves deep sexual expression of one another. The spouse delighting in cheating-Adultery due to migration or whatever the case may be is a very serious issue in marriage.

Healing from infidelity in marriage takes time, longer, probably, than it did to build the relationship in the first place. The trust is gone, and it might be rebuilt, one act of faith at a time. Even if your mate has forgiven what you did, that doesn't mean he or she will ever forgot that you strayed.

Marriage is not all about sex and children but also companionship. Companionship is one of the important basic needs of man. A man is motivated when he feels trusted and respected. Man/woman wants more than anything a soul mate and friend, someone loving, caring, and affectionate. Someone tender to talk to and have fun with. Someone who can be there for you, take interest in the things you do, trust, respect, be loyal and admire you. The ideal companion would focus on your good qualities more than your faults. Someone you could share your feelings, thoughts, interests and whole being. Someone you can relate and listen to with excitement without boundaries.

Commitment in Marriage

Husbands and wives who are committed to their marriage view it as a permanent bond, and that creates a sense of security between them. Each spouse is confident that the other will honor the union, even in difficult times.

Some couples feel compelled to stay together because of social or family pressure. Far better, however, is a sense of commitment that is based on mutual love and respect.

If you are committed to your marriage, you allow yourself to be wronged. You are quick to forgive and quick to apologize. You view problems as obstacles, not as deal breaker-Micah.

"When confronted with problems, spouses without commitment are likely to conclude, 'We just weren't made for each other' and look for ways to get out of the marriage.

Many people go into marriage knowing that they have a 'fallback plan'- divorce. When people enter marriage already thinking about the possibility of divorce, their commitment is lacking right from the start"-Jean.

Solution

You could ask yourself:

- Do you find yourself regretting that you married your spouse?
- Do you day dream about being with someone else?
- Do you say things such as "I'm leaving you"?
  Or "I'm going to find someone who appreciates me"?
  If you answered yes to one or more of those questions, now is the time to strengthen your commitment.
  Ask yourself: Has the level of commitment in our marriage decreased? If so, why?
  What steps can we take now to strengthen our commitment?

Way out

- Write an occasional love note to your spouse
- Show your commitment by displaying photos of your spouse on your desk at work
- Phone your spouse each day while you are at work or apart.

TEAMWORK

When there is teamwork in a marriage, a husband and wife are like a pilot and copilot with the same flight plan. Even when challenges arise, each spouse thinks in terms of 'we' rather than 'me'.

Marriage is not a solo act. Husband and wife must work together to make it successful-Christopher.

When a conflict arises a husband and wife who are not a team will tend to attack each other rather than the problem. Minor issues will turn into major obstacles.

Imagine a tennis match with two of you on opposite sides of the net. Instead, what practical steps can you take to join your spouse so that you are both on the same team dancing?

Instead of thinking, 'How can I win?' think 'How can we both win?' Forget about who is right and who is wrong. That isn't as important as having peace and unity in your marriage.-Ethan.

Respect

Respectful spouses care about each other even during a disagreement. 'These couples don't get gridlocked in their separate position, 'says the book Ten Lessons to transform your Marriage.' "Instead, they, keep talking with each other about conflicts. They listen respectfully to their spouses' perspectives and they find compromises that work for both sides.' To respect your wife means that you appreciate her values and you don't want to do anything that would damage her or your marriage.-Brian.

Check

Ask yourself;

- How often did I give criticize my spouse, and how often did I give her a compliment?
- In what specific ways did I show respect for my spouse?
- What actions and words would help each of you feel respected?
- What actions and words make each of you feel disrespected?

To respect your husband means showing it by your actions that you value him and that you want him to be happy. It isn't always a grand gesture; sometimes a series of small acts can demonstrate genuine respect"-Megan. In the end, it is not a matter of whether you view yourself as respectful or not; it is a question of whether your spouse feels respected. Be compassionate, tender, kindness, humility, mildness and patience are important.

Forgiveness

To forgive means that you let go of an offense and any feelings of resentment it may have caused. Forgiveness does not require that you minimize the wrong or pretend it never occurred. Forgive freely and as many times you are wronged. "When you love someone, you look past that person's imperfections and instead see the person that he or she is trying to become-Aaron.

If you hold on to resentment, you can harm yourself physically and emotionally-you can also damage your marriage.

"One time my husband apologized for something that hurt me deeply. It was hard for me to forgive him. I eventually did, but I regret that I didn't do it sooner. It put an unnecessary strain on our relationship,"-Julia.

When you are offended, do not attribute bad motives to your spouse. Try to excuse your spouse's behavior, remembering that" we all stumble many times"

It's easy to forgive when we're both at fault, but it's more difficult when the offense seems one-sided. Accepting an apology and forgiving takes true humility-Kimberly.

If you hold unto resentment, you can harm yourself physically and emotionally- you can also damage your marriage.

SHOW APPRECIATION

It's easy to get too comfortable in a relationship, and sometimes that comfort can translate into forgetting to show your partner respect and appreciation. Dr. Edelman says our partners can feel taken for granted if we don't tell them we like what they're doing for us. "It means a lot when you acknowledge the large and small things they do for you," Dr. Edelman says. "Say, 'Thanks for making breakfast today. I really appreciate all the time you saved me. It means a lot because I know you were really busy today.'"

LEARN FROM WHAT YOU THINK IS HIS MISTAKE

Instead of harping on a mental list of things your partner does that secretly drive you crazy, find a way to learn from what makes them different from you. "This resolution will cause you to think outside the box about how you consider a trait or behavior good versus bad," says Kyrss Shane, a LMSW and mental health professional. "It will also challenge you to turn an annoyance into something beneficial, helping you not to be bothered by that trait and helping your partner to not feel that this trait is a negative part of who they are."

GIVE YOUR TIME TO ONE ANOTHER

It's easy to spend a handful of minutes, or even an hour or two, on your phone without even realizing it. But giving your full attention to the screen in front of you, instead of your partner, can lead to problems in the relationship. Jill Murray, Ph.D., a licensed psychotherapist, suggests making next year the year when you both vow to stay off your phones when you're together. "So many couples go out to dinner and both of them are face down looking at their phones, absorbed in social media," says Murray. "They are 'liking' other people's lives more than they are liking their partner. Commit to giving your focus and attention to your partner."

HANDLE ARGUMENTS PROPERLY.

No couple is immune to arguments, and having a system in place to handle hurt feelings now will strengthen your relationship later. Matthew Mutchler, Ph.D., LMFT, says he often sees couples who have different expectations of how to handle a disagreement. "People get wrapped up in being 'right' or 'fixing' a problem [and] they miss the point," says Mutchler. "Underlying many conflicts is a desire to be heard, understood, and validated. You can tell the quality of a relationship by how they hear and respond to one another. Your partner might just want you to say 'I understand what you're feeling' without qualifications.

SHARE NEW EXPERIENCES TOGETHER

Relationships thrive when good communication exists, but for that to happen, both people need to know how to speak each other's language. "If you have something emotional to say, try to keep it simple so your partner is less likely to get overwhelmed," says Dr. Susan Edelman, a board-certified psychiatrist. "Use 'I language': Say, 'I feel' rather than 'you always,' which can feel like an accusation. If your partner criticizes you, try to hear their concern even if you feel defensive.

CHAPTER 3

NUCLEAR FAMILY

A nuclear household consists of a married couple and their unmarried children, or a single parent and unmarried children; whereas an extended household comprises, in addition to a nuclear family unit, a broader set of kin and sometimes unrelated individuals.

This nuclear group is found worldwide, but it is most prevalent in the west where it seems to epitomize the modern family. In a western country such as the UK, little more than a quarter of all households are nuclear families.

Nuclear families are commonest in industrialized cities, with the advent of Industrialization, adult life expectancy increased, so three generation families become common in towns and cities.

In Africa, nuclear families are in the minority, this is because men leave their wife and children in search of money, passion and power. On getting there they are grabbed by younger ladies anxiously looking for already made men. Having in mind that men are free to marry as many wives as possible but for a woman, one man is enough, you have to stick to your first husband till death do you part, even if he is beating you up you have your children to take care of, you must listen and obey your husband, you can be the first wife which is the only honor you have as a married woman. Tolerant, the elders will tell you.

Once the man goes out, he might not come back to his first wife again, he would pretend to be charmed, forgetful and searching for useless reasons for his actions. The irresponsible man now gives reasons for abandoning his young beautiful wife and children he once loved and suffered with when they had nothing but love for a new illegal cohabitation.

IMPACT OF MIGRATION ON THE NUCLEAR FAMILY

This entails greater reliance by the abandoned and the children, a weakening of wider kinship relationships and a consequent widening of the roles of nuclear family members especially women. (Migration and Family, p.48)Female headship of incomplete nuclear families is common in areas where temporary mobility occurs. In such circumstances women and children must perform tasks naturally done by men. (Nalm (53), p.425) found that the extended absences of Minaugkabau migrant men from their homes created strains within family and may have been responsible for an unusually high incidence of Oedipus complex among children and of mental disorders among women.

Families of migrant men at the place of origin must adjust not only to the permanent or temporary absence of family members, but also to the influences of the newly acquired money, goods, ideas, attitudes, behavior and innovations transmitted back to them by the movers. This is because the acquired position, money, power have a great influence on the mover, who are dominantly the men.

Migration of the head of the family does lead to the separation of family members, creating a greater dependence on the nuclear family, weakening wider kinship relationships and consequently expanding the roles of nuclear family members, especially the women. Caldwell 8 (21) p. 274) has identified such changes as being critical to the transition from high to low fertility, which requires a reversal of the net flow of wealth.

Hattaway (25) p.3) suggests that the mobility induced separation of family members, even for short periods, leads to marital instability and the consequent permanent break-up of the family unit, whereas Gonzalex (21), p.1266) cites several studies of the societies in which the temporary separation of husband and wife has been consistent with marital instability. A high incidence of divorce among the Mainangkabau of Western Sumatra has been attributed to high rates of male migration (53) p.426), whereas Lineton (44), p.65) suggests that the low incidence of divorce among the Bugis of Wajo is partly because nuclear families migrate as a whole.

Though in more recent years, increased modernization and industrialization has generally led to families becoming more geographically and socially mobile, with the result that extended family ties are shed. Modern industrial and urban living is tending to erode family structures back into the more isolated nuclear form. The more that families become isolated from their grandparents and other relatives, the more they become reliant on state and private support.

Migration of the man/head of the household to another country in search of greener pasture is becoming a big issue in families. The nuclear family is most affected, the wife and children would be left behind to suffer and to take care of themselves. The burden would be on the woman of the house/wife, this is because she would be depressed hoping for the husband to be back, the extended family would begin to look into her family affairs monitor and control her. They would want to know how she gets the finance for her family needs and begin to label her "a prostitute……."

The 'Girl Child' in every family should be educated before giving her out in marriage. If the 'girl child' is educated, she would be able to take care of her family in the absence of the husband. She stands a better chance of sending her children to school to be well educated because she would have a good job, soon she would catch up with her new role and responsibility as a single parent and head of her family.

Having a man or no man in your life does not define whom you are as a person. You have just one life to live, you need to make yourself happy as much as you can. You should not allow yourself to be put down because of the absence of a man that does not want nor love you. Move on with your life and enjoy it, you have a great destiny to fulfill.

Soon the single parent would get used to her new roles and be strong to take care of herself and her children. When men migrate they begin to form another nuclear family over there and tend to forget their first love, this is ridiculous. It would be like a dream to her, she might fall sick, depressed, crying most of the time, emotionally, socially, psychologically and physically down. The family is separated, divorced and irreparable. Children are disorganized, growing up without the father figure in their lives which was not what the woman anticipated when she got married. Family disintegration affects children more because the boys would join bad people that would teach them to smoke, fight, become a school dropout and many more ills, while the girls will tend to experiment on sex and thereby have babies without father when they are babies themselves.

These days when a man wants to migrate, he would sit with the wife to discuss, it's either your family goes with you or forget it. Disintegration of families is not the best for the family, church, society, community nor the country.

DANGER OF ALCOHOLISM

IMPACT OF SUBSTANCE ABUSE ON FAMILIES

It is important to understand that family with an alcoholic member" has alcoholism' in the same way that families with a mental or physical illness are impacted by those illness. Alcoholism regulates all behaviors in the family life.

Therefore, if the primary regulatory relationship in the family is with alcohol or drugs, then other relationships in the family become secondary and do not prosper as well as in a family without alcohol, tobacco and drug abuse.

Denial is an integral component of the abused family homeostasis mechanism, the family will blame factors outside of the family for their problems (i.e. loss of job, lack of money, problems at work/school, argument with friend). This externalization of blame reflects the powerlessness felt throughout the family system. The chemically dependent member functions to bring the family together as they bond against these outside issues through the crises that are caused by the abuse (Fisher & Harrison, 1997).

Families with substance abuse problems utilize criticism, anger, blame, guilt and judgment in the family communication process as is seen in the marital dyad. Parenting is inconsistent, and the boundaries are nuclear and consistently changing (Lowery, 1998). A study shows that the most common consequences were distress at witnessing violence to the other parent or to the home, verbal abuse toward the children, feelings of shame, and taking on caring and protective roles. However, the children were not passive victims and usually took active steps to tackle the drinking or modify its impact.

Many abused families wished they could meet with others in the same position, so they could feel less isolated and learn from each other. There is need for network of services with group work, individual counseling, family meditation and educational components to keep the family together and moving forward.

Parental alcoholism appears to create the same type of dysfunction that exists in families with sexual, physical, or emotional abuse. This makes the children in these families at high risk for the development of a variety of stress- related disorders (Kelly & Myers, 1996), including conduct disorders, poor academic performance, and inattentiveness. Children in substance abuse families are socially immature, lack self-esteem and self- efficacy, and have deficits in social skills (Sales, 2000). All these leads to family dysfunction in so many ways, in which case the father moves away, living irresponsible life and wife lives as a single mother taking care of the children alone. This is actually a family drama issue.

CHAPTER 4

VIOLENCE AGAINST WOMEN

INTRODUCTION

Domestic violence is the willful intimidation, physical assault, battery, sexual assault and or other abusive behavior as part of perpetrated by one intimate partner against another. It includes physical violence, sexual violence, physical violence, and emotional abuse.

Violence manifests within the family, in the home or in interpersonal relationships, and is inclusive of abuse, rape and sexual abuse. It also covers violence in the community, including rape, sexual abuse, torture, trafficking and forced prostitution, kidnapping and sexual harassment in work place, in educational and health care institutions and other settings. Violence exercised by people or private institutions is also a violation of international law.

Violence against women takes many forms, from physical attacks to mental assault, including verbal abuse, extreme possessiveness or harassment. Physical attack is often accompanied by sexual violence.

A recent UN survey found that in countries as diverse as Kuwait, Samoa, Uganda, Chile, Poland and the US, violence against women is greatly exacerbated by alcohol and drug abuse. The majority of women are targets of violence in their role as wife or lover, but they are also victims as daughters, daughter-in-law, sisters, sisters-in-law, ex-wives, ex-lovers and mothers.

Since the frequency and intensity of attacks usually escalates with time, the longer a woman is victimized, the more likely she is to be seriously hurt or killed. Crime statistics from Canada show that 60% of all women murdered between 1961 and 1974 were killed within the family. Research from Thailand, Kenya, Bangladesh and Australia shows similar results, (The troubled Family by Boyden pp.99)

Many criminologists believe that domestic violence against women is the most underreported crime. In incest cases especially, victims tend to feel humiliated and shamed, and sometimes guilty. Usually they choose to put up with abuse rather than risk family breakup or social ostracism. Even when women and children do speak up, few people are prepared to listen or take them seriously. (Boyden, pp. 99)

It is necessary to recognize that gender based violence violates women's fundamental rights, which include the right to life, liberty and protection from discrimination and gender inequality as well as freedom of thought and the right not to be tortured.

Gender- based violence is understood as an obstacle to the full realization of women's potential and an impediment to their total participation in every sphere of life. As indicated in the Program of Action from the International Conference on Population and Development (Cairo, 1994) and the Beijing Conference (1995), gender-based violence is harmful to reproductive health.

The convention is also applicable to those practice by institutions and health services that do not respect women's physical, social and moral integrity. To this end, medical treatment and experimentation are prohibited without the woman's consent. Respect for her body and her decisions are the foundation for the elimination of violence.

DOMESTIC VIOLENCE

Domestic violence is when one person does a variety of things to control another in an intimate relationship. Most people wonder if what is happening to them is domestic violence because their partner has never hit them. Physical abuse is probably what most people think of when they think about domestic violence, but it is just one of the many ways that your partner might try to gain power and control in your relationship.

This is a woman's night mare. African women honor and obey their husbands, hold them in high esteem because it's inculcated in them from childhood, but men have turned it to dishonor and constant beating. A 1997 study found that domestic violence is common in all regions and spans, all social classes and groups in the country, it results in significant physical, psychological and social impairment of women.

The crises of domestic violence is intensified by social and legal constructions of the family as "private" and popular perceptions of male power as normative. This fuels the universal ideology of male supremacy that bestows on men the obligation and prerogative to chastise their wives.

Regardless of social beliefs and ideologies about gender and family relations, the prospect of prohibiting and punishing domestic violence depends, foremost, on the state's willingness and capacity to reform criminal and family laws. Though the Nigerian constitution guarantees equal rights to all citizens, including clauses that bar discrimination on the basis of sex, it is still not enough to deter domestic violence.

At the Nigerian National Assembly a draft bill on domestic violence was not too long ago introduced, but it is inadequate because it merely addresses violence against women and not domestic violence. For what it is worth, maybe they should bring criminal law to bear on some aspects of intra-family violence and establish prohibitions and punishments for violence between family members.

SEXUAL VIOLENCE

A husband's sexual violence is generally a taboo topic and so women victims feel anguished, fearful and ashamed of admitting it. A woman may be able to admit to being beaten, but to acknowledge that the man also forces her to have sex may cause her so much pain that it becomes the most difficult trauma to admit. This also includes making you engage in sexual acts that make you uncomfortable; forcing you to engage in prostitution.

PSYCHOLOGICAL VIOLENCE

Psychological violence provokes serious deterioration of the affected person's mental health, sometimes driving them to suicide. The higher rate of suicide does not overtly appear to be related to a violent situation, but the links may become clear when the case is further investigated.

A husband can destroy his wife psychologically, leave her isolated, prevent her from working, refuse to give her money and discredit her, calling her names, putting her down or embarrassing her in front of other people, criticizing your abilities as a partner or parent. In such cases, physical violence becomes superfluous.

Women seek medical treatment because of the anxiety violence provokes, and they are given tranquilizers. Then, when the husband comes home, they take the pills so as not to 'provoke' him. The medication makes them more vulnerable, and they are less able to escape from a violent situation. The experience of constant fear has a tremendous impact. It brings on emotional and psychological instability. A person who lives in expectation and fear of severe physical or psychological harm is incapable of visualizing himself in an alternative scenario.

Abused women generally visit medical Doctors because of their physical symptoms, because they are anxious or because they themselves are more violent with the children. A woman can be in therapy for years without ever stating that her real problem is violent. That is why it is so important to educate health professionals about this issue.

It is also necessary to train the professionals responsible for initial treatment. They need to overcome the myths which make it difficult to perceive women's real needs. They must examine their own experiences with violence, their own family histories and ask themselves why they fail to consider certain types of behavior as violent.

PHYSICAL VIOLENCE

Battered women experience a variety of physical problems which could indicate that they are living in a violent situation. The physical symptom is similar to those who live through prolonged periods of stress. The constant threat of life generates a level of stress sometimes impossible to bear. Physical violence includes- pushing, grabbing, hitting, slapping, punching, or kicking you.

MINIMIZING, DENYING, BLAMING

This is done by making you think the abuse is your fault; saying the abuse was caused by stress, alcohol, or problems at work; it's your parents fault to divide his family; he was spiritually attacked by his anniversaries against his marriage; denying that the abuse happened at all.

USING CHILDREN

This includes- undermining your authority with your children; threatening to take the children away from you by kidnapping or getting custody of them; "pumping" your children for information about you to change, hate you and love him.

COERCION AND THREAT

This includes- showing you a weapon and threatening to use it on you; threatening to pastes your naked/ nude pictures on Facebook; threatening to harm your family, friends, or anyone you might go to for help.

LONELY SINGLE LADY

ISOLATION

It includes- making it hard for you to see your friends and family; telling you that your friends and family cause problems in the relationship or are trying to" come between you"; cutting you off from people that care about you, your uncles, aunties, relations.

WORDS OF ENCOURAGEMENT/COMFORT TO DOMESTIC VIOLENCE SURVIVORS DELIVERED BY BEATRICE NWALOZIE ON OCTOBER, 2014 ANNIVERSARY, AT BARRIER FREE LIVING, MANHATTAN, NEW YORK.

Learn to turn your pain into purpose your messes into your message and your hurt into hope. Find peace and purpose in the hurts of your past. Using what you've gone through to minister to someone, that is true freedom. Your wounds need to heal and become scars.

Don't revenge: Revenge means you are fighting your own battle and God becomes a spectator in your battle field. No, let God fight it. Let go, hand over your pain, hurting, cries and all your loneliness over to Him and have your peace. God sees, knows, understands and will handle them all, victory and peace would be yours at last.

Refuse to lose hope at all as you journey through life. <u>Determination and Hope</u> are your passports to success. You need to be alive to see your dream come through, stop that worrying, bitterness and move on. Strive to cultivate the cheerful, hopeful disposition that will enable you see the silver lining to every dark cloud. Let the abuser see and hear of your progress/success.

Never pity yourself, your background, age or your level of education, move further from where you stopped. Keep HOPE ALIVE. Hope is the great echo of the spirit in us. All that you hope for by the grace of Almighty God you shall have them.

No matter what challenges you face today, take comfort that the Almighty God knows every issue on your heart and is able to shoulder your burdens. Hold fast to the faithful one. Your challenges do not fall outside the scope of God's ability to intervene. God is mysterious, He's powerful and will see you through.

When you lift your eyes from your situation and fix them on your Savior- when you choose to trust Him-you will find peace in pain and strength in the struggle. (Excerpt from Girlfriends in God)

My motto: This too shall pass.

TIPS FOR THE DAY:

    a. Avoid negative friends, stick to positive ones;
    b. Be the most honest person you know;
    c. Use your life to make the world a better place;
    d. Daily have 7 minutes of quiet time with God;
    e. Stop the blame game and move on;
    f. Don't be lazy, find something doing;
    g. Exercise yourself daily, it helps;

h.   Do what makes you happy;

i.   When no one else believes in your vision, keep it up, have the courage to on and be resourceful;

j.   Change is hard at the beginning, messy in the middle and gorgeous a end. Change comes with progress;

k.   Delete victim speeches from your vocabulary, like' No more, I can't mak It's not possible', Why me', It's so bad, Hard……Rather say, 'I will, I make it, 'this is awesome. Fabulous and great', what's the opportunity h Etc.;

l.   Inspire someone today;

m.   Living in the past is disrespecting your future;

n.   Smile at people when you see them, say, please to respect them and t you to appreciate them;

o.   Be focus, goal setting, no procrastination;

p.   Remember that your greatest gift is so much stronger than your deepest (Excerpt from inspiration independent awakening)

Thank you for listening.

Beatrice.

CHAPTER 5

SINGLE PARENTS – LONE CAREERS. HOUSEHOLD HEADED BY WOMEN

This CHAPTER explores the prevalence of female headships and some of its demographic characteristics. A man's relation as a husband does not define whom you are as a person, this means, you need to study yourself and live a satisfactory and fulfilling life that makes you happy at all times.

Today, between one-quarter and one third of all households are headed by single parents. Lone parenthood has always been a part of family life. In the past, early death in adulthood was one of its main causes. It could also be caused by frequent wars or epidemics; many were widowed, three or four times.

Today, high rates of separation and divorce, migration and births to women without partners are the major causes of single-parent families. Most people are driven into single parenthood, but for many it is only a temporary arrangement until they remarry.

Life is difficult for single parents, especially the single mothers, not least because of prejudice and social stigma. The sheer physical and emotional fatigue of raising children alone and trying to be the main source of both affection and authority at the same time, drains morale.

Lone teenage mothers are more vulnerable because early child-bearing can cause health complications, poverty and social rejection. Lone fathers fare better than lone mothers because friends, relatives and neighbors are more likely to rally around to help.

Research has shown that nine out of every ten lone parents are women. Men can move more freely in and out of parenting relationships than women; they can decline involvement in the maintenance, nurture, and upbringing of their children. In many cultures, male partners are often transient members of the household.

In wealthier parts of the world, some economically independent women are now choosing parenthood without a partner. To these women, single parenthood presents new challenges and new opportunities. In Africa and in Nigeria in particular, men drift to the cities in search of employment, leaving their young beautiful wives and children behind without any remorse. A few send remittances, but a good number do not.

Compared to males, female householders are disadvantaged in many ways. They are more likely to be the head of the household due to circumstances, rather than choice. In the developing world, they married when young- their husbands were four to eight years older, on an average- so they are less experienced in the ways of the world and less educated. It is far more difficult for women to maintain their families than men because they have less access to the market economy. When they do earn, their wages are generally far lower than men's.

BUSY SINGLE MOTHER

SOCIAL AND ECONOMIC FACTORS ASSOCIATED WITH THE EMERGENCE OF FEMALE HEADED HOUSEHOLDS

Most studies focus on the recent emergence of households maintained by females and their influence on the welfare of women and their children. Available evidence reveals that female headship was not uncommon in some cultures in the past. Having a woman as household has been documented as a tradition in some African societies. For example, in Kwahu, a society in Ghana, a matrilineal descent group with a depth of about four generations is most significant social group, with women running their daily subsistence (Bleek, 1987)

Among the possible reasons for the recent increase in female headship is male migration, leaving women as household's heads. During men's absence, by this instance women migrate in search of employment to take care of the children abandoned by the irresponsible man, women often become household's heads in the place of destination.

In countries of Eastern and Southern Africa, young men were the first to accept wage employment on white-owned firms and mines, fostering male out-migration and a concomitant increase in female headship. In the Caribbean, slavery stripped African men of authority over women and children. As a result, informed marriages became widespread in the region,

VULNERABILITY OF CHILDREN

Globally, many children take to living on the streets where they are persecuted and harassed by the police, shopkeepers, and local residents. These hungry and sick children are often drawn into drug and prostitution rings, the latter with the risk of unwanted pregnancies, backstreet abortion and infection from sexually transmitted diseases. They 'belong' to nobody, and children living without adults are easy prey-there is no one to defend them or to mourn their death, this is the plight of 'child-headed families' they are the most vulnerable family unit.

MOTHER/CHILD CO RESIDENCE, BY MOTHER'S MARITAL STATUS

The chances of a child living apart from the mother differ sharply according to the mother's marital status. Children are most likely to be living with mothers who are currently in their first marital union, regardless of the children's age. For very young children (Less than 5-18 years old), the divorced or separated group of mother usually have the highest percentage living or residing with their mothers in developing countries.

Increasing urbanization and industrialization have caused greater number of women to change the nature of their work and to seek cash-earning activities. Even if they are low paid or insecure, the increasing labor force participation of women is likely to increase the total household income and to affect its expenditures. A large fraction of women in developing countries are working mothers owing to the combination of economic pressure and relatively high fertility

When maternal employment means long hours away from home, with little help for childcare, an overall negative impact on children can be expected. Maternal work outside the home would reduce the mother's time available to spend with her children. Mother's work might affect infants feeding practices and nutritional status of children, especially, when the children are small. Children ensure their parents' acceptance within their families and communities.

Indeed, several studies have demonstrated that maternal employment can have a positive effect on child's welfare, Women's paid job increases the overall family income, which benefits all family members, and including young children (Tucker, 1989; United Nations, 1992) other authors argue that more of women's income compared to men's income is spent on child- oriented expenses such as food, clothing and education.

CHAPTER 6

FAMILY MATTERS

The family is but one of many relationships making up the society, which is unique. This section shows why the family is so different: how it binds its members in a web of social, legal and economic ties- and also with powerful emotional bonds.

The family itself changes with the birth and nurture of the young, their growth to adulthood, and ageing of the founding members. But always it is a living tie between men and women, young and old. It explores the ever- increasing concern for the rights and wellbeing of the individual, especially the more vulnerable family members. Each individual in a family affects and influences the other, the wellbeing of one affects the other.

Today, the economic and social future of children in the poor and the middle class is being undermined by a culture that promotes teenage sex, divorce, cohabitation, and out-of-wedlock birth. Mary E. Williams, said that: "The root cause of poverty and disparity is linked undeniably to the presence or absence of marriage in our society, that almost half of American families are experiencing poverty following a divorce." "Three-fourths of all women applying for welfare benefits do so because of a disruption of marriage in America.

There are reports that children often suffer badly from a parental breakup or divorce, and those raised by a single parent usually perform poorly in their studies, suffer bad health and fall into addiction, crime and poverty in adulthood. The study unveiled that children whose parents split when they were between five and 16 years old had higher possibilities of developing an emotional disorder and a conduct disorder.

The research findings say that the family backgrounds of children are as important as the health, income and educational qualifications of their households.

Children from broken homes experience a hard time finishing school and finding a job, says (Stephen Lunn of News Corp Australian). Studies show that these children have higher tendencies of entering into multiple live-in relationships upon reaching adulthood. However, girls from divorced families are more likely to become teenage mothers. Children from divorced families engage in de facto relationships instead of marriage as a means of self- protection to avoid social and economic risks related to marriage.

MEN AND WOMEN

Men and women all over the world need to belong to a home, and a family which is your identity where you can easily be located. The marital bond is not only expected to fulfill the needs of the individual. Society, too, benefits from it for thousands of years, marriage has provided an ideal opportunity to forge alliances between groups, as to secure the future with heirs. It is more than a bond between husband and wife.

One ancient solution is marriage between cousins, which remains popular in Africa, (Nigeria) and Asia. In some regions of Pakistan and India, up to half of all marriages are between cousins, this will keep their wealth within their family circle. While marrying your cousin is banned in 30 States of the US, and is a criminal offence in eight of them. (Boyden, 1997).

WOMEN'S WORK AND MEN'S WORK

Actually, there may not always have been inequality between the sexes. In prehistoric times, women were esteemed because of their special relationship with nature: they created new life; grew most of the food. Their qualities were the first human ones to be revered in a religious way. Women's work in raising children, producing food, and keeping the home suffered a loss of status in their bid to securing a white collar job. With men's general monopoly of paid and mechanized labor, official statistics sometimes make it look as if women are not working at all.

The burden of family life which falls mostly on women and their role in producing the goods on which families depend for their survival is often ignored. In many parts of Sub-Saharan Africa, for example, women undertake the arduous and heavy agricultural work, in addition to the bearing, caring of children, running home and family life.

Some people mistakenly believe that little gender inequality exists nowadays. However, surveys and statistics show that women are still economically disadvantaged in the workplace as well as in the home-where they tend to work more hours than their male partners even if they also work full time.

CHAPTER 7

MEN AND FATHERS

Romancing and honoring your wife is one of the most important things you can do for your children. It's something they need to see you doing. The respect they have for you will skyrocket when they watch you helping her around the house and doing things like massaging her feet. Your children are watching to see how you treat her and others. When they see your sincere, kind demonstrations of affection toward your wife, they'll know they can expect to be treated well too. Make romancing your wife a ritual and watch your children respond and watch your wife response.

Never derogate or talk down to your wife, especially in front of your kids. Instead build her up with praises on a constant basis. Don't be fooled, our children hear every word and they notice how you treat one of their two most favorite people. A father must find a way to balance being both parent and friend to their kids. You must build genuine friendships with your kids if you are going to be approachable and have a lasting impact on their lives. Henry Ward Beecher, said: "There is no friendship, no love like that of the parents for the child."

Men's own image of themselves as husbands and fathers and the expectations of them, vary considerably and within cultures. Generally, many men do not have the authority to be loving and caring fathers, and are physically absent from their children for a variety of reasons, such as separation, divorce, deliberate irresponsibility, or migration to cities or other countries in search of work/high pay and great living environment.

Even when living in the same home, most men are absent from the process of rearing their young children. As countries industrialize, the role of fathers in families becomes increasingly tied to works away from home; their role as a socializer of children declines. Studies tend to confirm the male tendency to identify more with the 'provider' role than the 'nurturer' role, and many feel inadequate in the "women's domain" of child care and development. George Forman said "Fatherless homes are at epidemic proportions. As a result there's a whole generation of kids who lack direction." But generally, children who grow up in a stable, two-parent family have the best prospects for achieving income security as adults.

You must defend, protect, sacrifice, make unpopular decisions, take the pressure, and carry the load, while at the same time being loving, wise and understanding. Successful fatherhood seems an impossible task. Well, the truth is, it is impossible........impossible without the help of the good Lord. God gives wisdom, knowledge and encouragement, when you neglect God, your family is in jeopardy.

PARENTING

Communicating with children

"We need to assure our children that their feelings are important to us. If they think otherwise, they will keep their concerns locked inside or turn elsewhere for help.-Maranda.

"Don't overreact, even if your child's thinking is way off center"- Anthony.

Take advantage of informal setting when they're ready to open up. Sometimes children open up when they are not sitting face–to –face with a parent. "We take advantage of car rides. Being side-by-side rather than across from each other has led to good discussions"-Nicole

Mealtime presents another opportunity for informal conversation.

"At dinnertime each of us relates the worst thing and the best thing that happened that day. This practice unites us and lets each of us know that we don't have to face problems alone-Robin.

Discipline

The word Discipline can mean to guide or to teach. At times, that includes correcting a child's misbehavior. Often, though, it involves imparting moral training that helps a child learn to make good choices in the first place.

In recent decades, discipline has all but disappeared from some households, as parents fear that correction might lower a child's self-esteem. However, wise parents set reasonable rules and train their children to abide by them.

"Children need boundaries to help them grow into well-rounded adults. Without discipline, children are like a rudderless ship- which will eventually go off course or even capsize.-Pamela.

As Parents:

- Be Consistent, If your child does not adhere to your rules, enforce consequences. On the other hand, readily commend your child when he or she complies.
- "I frequently commend my children for their being obedient in a world where obedience is so rare. Commendation makes it easier for them to accept correction when it is needed,"-Christiane.
- Be Reasonable. Balance the child's age and competency level with the weight of the infraction. Consequences are usually most effective when they are related to the wrong- for example, misuse of phone might result in loss of phone privileges for a period of time. At the same time, avoid making major issues over minor irritations. "T try to determine if my child has been deliberately disobedient or if he just made an error in judgment. There is a difference between a serious trait that needs to be weeded out and a mistake that just needs to be pointed out".-Wendell.
- Be Loving. Discipline is much easier for children to accept and apply when they know that a parent's primary motive is love. "When our son made mistakes, we reassured him that we were proud of all the good decisions he had made in the past. We explained that the mistake wouldn't define him as long as made the needed correction and that we were there to help him do that."-Daniel. Discipline guides a child the way a rudder steers a boat and keeps it on course.

Trustworthy

Trustworthy people earn the confidence of their parents, friends and employers. They abide by the rules, keep their promises, and always tell the truth. Certainly, the amount of freedom you receive is directly related to the level of trust you have earned over time.

"The best way to earn your parents' trust is to demonstrate that you are mature and responsible, not only when you are with them but also when they are not around."-Sarahi.

To earn more trust;

Be honest. Nothing will shatter others' trust in you quicker than lies. Conversely, when you are open and honest-especially about your mistakes-you can earn the trust of others. "It's easy to be honest when things are going well, but being honest about things that cast you in a bad light goes a long way in building trust."-Caiman.

Be dependable. In on US. Survey, 78 percent of human-resource professionals indicate that reliability was "one of the three most important skills for entry-level positions". Learning to be dependable now will benefit you as an adult.

"My parents noticed when I'm responsible and do my chores without their having to nag me. The more I show initiative like that, the more they reward it with their trust."-Sarah.

Be patient. Unlike physical growth, which is readily apparent to others, time is often needed for others to recognize emotional and mental growth. "There's no single act that can earn the trust of your parents and others. But you can build it gradually if you're consistently responsible over time".-Brandon.

Goal setting- Goals are like blueprints; with effort, you can turn them into reality.

A goal is more than just a dream- something you wish would happen. Real goals involve planning, flexibility, and good, old-fashioned hard work. Goals can be short-range (taking days or weeks to accomplish), medium-range (months), and long-range (a year or more). Long-range goals can be reached through a series of intermediate specific objectives.

Reaching goals can boost your confidence, strengthen your friendships and increase your happiness.

- Self-confidence: When you set small goals and reach them, you gain the confidence to take on bigger ones. You also feel more confident when facing day-to-day challenges- such as standing up to peer pressure.
- Friendships: people enjoy being around those who are reasonably goal-oriented-that is, those who what they want and are willing to work for it. Moreover, one of the best ways to strengthen a friendship is to work with another person toward a common goal.
- Happiness: When you set and reach goals, you feel a sense of accomplishment.

"I love having goals. They keep me occupied and give me something to keep reaching for. And when you reach a goal, it feels great to look back and say. Wow, I really did it! I accomplished what I set out to do". – Christopher. It's good to set a realistic goal and deadline, plan the steps involved, anticipate obstacles, and think of how to overcome them. Do not wait until you have every detail worked out to get started. Ask yourself, 'What is the very first thing I can do toward reaching my goal?' Track your progress as you complete each step with diligent.

TIME FATHER SPENT WITH CHILDREN

A study of four-year olds in 10 countries discovered that the average daily time spent alone by fathers with their children was less than one hour, ranging from 6 minutes per day in Hong Kong and 12 minutes in

Thailand to 50 minutes in China and 48 minutes in Finland. When the average time spent with both parents was added in, the number of hours father were present with their children ranged from 1 hour and 36 minutes in the US to 3 hours and 42 minutes in Belgium. These findings suggest that even fathers are present as an active member of a family, their direct involvement in child care can be very limited.

The nineteenth century ideal of the father was a remote but authoritarian figure. Fathers did much work at home before the industrial revolution and the family often worked together as an economic unit. The industrial revolution greatly enhanced man's authority in the home. With increase earning power, a man's status was marked by ability to provide for his wife and children. If his wife was force to work, he was thought to have failed as a man and as a husband. In most societies today, a man is expected by tradition and religion to' keep' his wife and children: to be the 'bread winner' and the head of the house. Fathers usually provide for the family and though they buy toys, they will rarely play with the children. They have to learn that interaction with their children is important and necessary. Research suggest, however, that there is a connection between lack of a father figure and problems such as delinquency and low academic achievement on children.

The industrial work ethic is hostile to fatherhood. Men's devotion to work and absence from the home is deemed to be natural. Men are expected to put their work first; the role of the father is seen in relation to work place. Few companies plan for their male employees to become fathers or grant paid paternity leave.

Concessions for mothers, such as childcare facilities at work, maternity leave are denied to fathers. Men and employers may need to re-evaluate their roles and responsibilities.

Media images of fatherhood have been undergoing a quiet revolution. In a study of the US media, it was found that the pre 1970 depiction of men as caregivers was of humbling, ineffective individuals. Today, this has changed to a potentially effective and important role in the social and emotional development of children. Also in the US, a magazine "Full-Time Dad" is published for care-giving fathers hoping to end the isolation that fathers who deeply care for their children often face. The joys and pleasures of nurturing children are a key feature of the magazine. Men who miss out on the nurturing role within a family miss some of the greatest joys in life.

Industrialization not only propelled man into higher status occupations; it also gave women paid employment. These days, many urban families cannot meet their material needs with a single income. Globally, women are becoming the majority sex in the workforce due to men's unemployment rate and job selection. Nowadays, the distribution of authority within the family is less clear than in the past. Increasingly, men and women must negotiate the terms of their partnership. Husbands may choose to stay at home to care for children if their wives have greater earning power: Few couples have the courage to adopt this life style in practice. In one U.S study, only 4 out of 3600 men cared for their children fulltime. Sweden is one of the few "father- friendly" countries. Swedish parents may take two months antenatal maternity leave, 10 days paternity leave, and a further 12 months parental leave which is paid to a level just below current income. The couple divide their leave as they wish, although only one parent can take leave at one time, but Swedish man take far less paternity leave than women.

Parenthood is physically exhausting, requiring patience, endurance and commitment. It is also uniquely rewarding and challenging, changing the way adults live and think. Children are a source of great happiness, fascination, and pride, such as when they take their first steps or babble their first words. They have a dramatic impact on the status of the marriage, too. Wedding toasts promise fertility and the personal fulfillment of having children.

BUILDING THE FAMILY

Both women and men should be given greater choice about how they balance their work and family lives. We all need to put hands on deck to make sure that family institution succeeds for future generation, we have been beneficiaries, to the gains derived from living and coming out from a family.

Modifying the organization of employment itself, both women and men may be given greater choice about how they balance their work and family lives. Employers can play their part by introducing flexible working schedules which include part time, job sharing, term-time and twilight shifts enabling parents and those with adult defendants to adjust work demands to home responsibly. Providing for career breaks such as maternity and paternity leave, without letting them jeopardize opportunities for promotion.

Emphasis can also be placed on assisting parents to re-enter the workforce by offering child care in the work place. Adapting the opening hours of service facilities such as health centers and child care can benefits family welfare.

The profit in using family, friendly measures far outweigh the cost: employers are able to retain skilled workers, attract a wider pool of applicants, reduce labor turnover, and match labor supply more effectively to demand. For women, family-friendly measures are vital. They improve access to employment, generally, and help to remove women's handicap in job market, since they are the ones who work part-time or leave employment for several years to raise the family.

Supportive employers can also provide positive options for men to help them create closer bonds with their children, and to force a climate of opinion in which men are seen as active parents sharing domestic responsibilities with women.

A family's income is used to finance immediate needs and, if it is sufficient, may allow the family to save for future needs. There are two elements in the amount of income received: the dollar value of hours worked and the number of hours worked. These in turn are affected by, among other things, the parents' education level and work habits that typically are formed in the early years. The relationship between poverty and the absence of intact marriages is indeed very strong.

25 qualities of husbands who love their wives by Author Dr. Robert Lewis:

1. Includes his wife in envisioning the future.
2. Accepts spiritual responsibility for his family.
3. He is willing to say "I'm sorry" and "Forgive me" to his family.
4. Discusses household responsibilities with his wife and makes sure they fairly distributed.
5. Seeks consultation from his wife on all major financing decisions.
6. Follows through with commitments he has made to his wife.
7. Anticipates the different stages his children will pass through.
8. Anticipates the different stages his marriage will pass through.
9. Frequently tells his wife what he likes about her.
10. Provides financially for his family's basic living expenses.
11. Deals with distraction so he can talk with his wife and family.
12. Prays with his wife on a regular basis.
13. Initiates meaningful family traditions.
14. Initiates fun family outings for the family on a regular basis.
15. Takes the time to give his children practical instruction about life.
16. Manages the schedule of the home and anticipates pressure points.
17. Keeps his family financially sound and out of harmful debt.
18. Makes sure he and his wife have drawn up a will.
19. Lets his wife and children into the interior of his life.
20. Honors his wife in public.
21. Explains sex to each child in a way that gives them a wholesome perspective
22. Encourages his wife to grow as an individual.
23. Takes the lead in establishing sound family values.
24. Provides time for his wife to pursue her own personal interests.
25. Is involved in a small group of men dedicated to spiritual growth.

The marriage of the parents has much to do with a child's educational attainment and work ethic. The relationship can be expressed as an equation: Income= (education attained) x (work ethic) x) unity of family structure)

..........Of course, one does not obtain an adequate and steady income just by marrying. Increasing the number of hours worked at a job valued by the marketplace will provide more income. The number of hours worked is linked directly to educational achievement and family structure. Families whose members have lower levels of education normally will have to work longer to reach a modest level of financial security than do those whose members achieve higher levels of education. Although the income of a family household depends on the educational level of parents, it is the parents' income rather than their level of education that predicts more accurately the level of education their children will achieve. In general, children with high- income parents receive more education than do children of lower income parents. Education gives the child from a high-income family a great advantage.

Today, social science research broadly characterizes the children who are most likely to attain a good income as adults: They have parents who are married; they finish school, get a job, abstain from inter-course until marriage, and marry before having children of their own. But family structure plays an even larger role in children's future prosperity than those who have formulated public policy over the past 30 years have been willing to admit. Having a baby out of wedlock usually derails progress toward achieving a stable family structure and income.

It is not that the number of babies born to teens has changed; it is that marriage within this group has vanished. In addition, almost half of the mothers of out-of-wedlock children will go on to have another child out of wedlock.

More than any other group, teenage mothers who give birth outside of marriage spend more of their lives as single parents. Not surprisingly, their children spend more time in poverty than do children of any other family structure. A single-parent family background and the poverty that usually accompanies it render children twice as likely to drop out of high school.

EPILOGUE

All through ages, the family remain both central and strong. For centuries it has withstood social catastrophes and revolutions- but it has remained unchanged by them. We are at a crossroads between what the family has been, and what it will become in the future. Childhood, parenthood, old age all are likely to be redefined. The emergence of a new political class of older people, for example, is just one issue families and governments still have to grapple with. As human society becomes more complex, so the great diversity of family lives and forms is expected to continue.

It is necessary for us to invest in families, if not we may pay a high price. For most individuals, the family is by far the most significant institution. Whether we grow up anxious or confident, trusting or suspicious, ambitious or contented is determined very largely by our early experiences of family life. Evils which a well-supported family and childhood can reduce or eliminate are as follows: addiction, ill health, crime, school drop-out rates and callous self-interest. Measures to tackle serious family crises-abandonment, abuse and neglect, and marital breakdown-are essential in all societies.

Protecting and empowering the family is of crucial importance if those future generations are to enjoy a decent quality of life. The family is the most fundamental resources for human society. Guaranteeing the transfer of resources between generations is fundamental to the notion of "sustainability". The present generation has a responsibility to future ones to provide a healthier, most secure environment for the family to act out its role in human society. Family is the fundamental bed rock of human beings.

BIBLIOGRAPHY

1. Boyden, J. Families (celebrate and hope in a world of change)
    Gala Books Ltd, 66 Charlotte Street, London
    WIPIR, 1993.

2. United Nations,
    Living Arrangements of "Women and their children
    In Developing Countries United Nations.
    Publication Sales No. E.96X11.5, 1995

3. Maria, M.
    Violence against Women. A United Nations
    Publication. Campaign for women'
    Human Rights, A life free of Violence

4. Basu, Alaka.
    Relationship of women's economic roles to child
    Health and well-being. Paper prepared for the United
    Nations experts group meeting on population and women,
    Gaborone, Botswana, 22-26 June, 1992

5. Bruce, Judith and Cynthia, B Lloyd (1992).
    Beyond female headship: Family research and policy issues for the 1990s. Paper presented at the workshop on Research. Methods 12-14 February, 1992. Washington. Finding the ties that bind beyond leadership and household. Working paper No.41. New York .The Population Council.

6. Ono-osaki, Keiko, (1991).
Female headed household in developing, countries: By choice or by circumstances. In demographic and health surveys world conference proceedings, Vol.111. Columbia Maryland: Institute for resource Development/Macro Systems, Inc., pp.1603-1622.

7. Violence against Women :(Pauline's Publications Africa Daughters of St Paul ISBN9966-21-321-x. 1997 edition. Nairobi-Kenya.)
8. Domestic Violence: New York State Office for the Prevention of Domestic Violence. (1996, 2000, 2008, 2010).
9. Counselling Skills for Dummies - A Wiley Brand. 2nd Edition by Gail Evans. (2013)
10. George Forman, Fatherhood (2008).
11. Poverty and Homeless, Mary, E. Williams. (2004).
12. Inner-City Poverty, Tamara L. Roleff (2003)
13. George Forman, Fatherhood (2008).
14. Poverty and Homeless, Mary, E. Williams. (2004).
15. Inner-City Poverty, Tamara L. Roleff (2003)
16. Substance Abuse Treatment and Family Therapy, A Treatment Improvement Protocol TIP 39 by SAMHA, 2004

BEATRICE NDUDIM GOLDSON-NWALOZIE is an Assistant Director (AD) in the Federal Ministry of Education, Abuja, Nigeria. She worked in the International Division of the Ministry in the Branch: Bilateral Agreement, Commonwealth, and African Affairs (BACAA) between Nigeria and every other Country in the field of Education.

She is good in: Writing Memorandum of Understanding (MOU), Agenda of meetings, drafting letters, Official Memos, Minutes of meetings and Reports of meetings, and Executive Summaries. Her schedule enabled her to represent Nigeria in many Bilateral Agreement meetings both within the country and outside. She has traveled to three Continents of the world and ten different Countries. She is well experienced in her Job, very intelligent and knowledgeable. Her work has been praised by many Ministers, Professors, Directors, Deputy Directors, Administrators and Colleagues.

Beatrice has Bachelor's Degree in Education/Biology and Master's Degree in Education Guidance and Counseling. She has taught students in High school for many years. She enjoys Writing, Mentoring, Tutoring, Teaching and Counseling. Now Beatrice lives in United States of America as a student and as an Author. She is a Counselor in the field of Drug and Substance Abuse (CASAC). She strongly believe Addiction is a disease and sobriety is possible. As an Author, her book has gone far and wide helping College students as a research reference book and families in standing out as an epitome of Peace and Happy family. She is writing her next book titled: "*DEN OF LOVE*", with subtitle there is "RINGING HOPE" for the Use.

Beatrice is an awesome Mom with three children, a Girl and two Boys. She is also a grandmother. **Beatrice** was married for twelve years, now a single parent. She has many Sisters and Brothers, Aunties and Uncles.

She is radiant, self-reliant, cheerful, friendly and charitable. In her free time she loves singing, watching soccer, visiting the sick to encourage and offer presents.

CPSIA information can be obtained
at www.ICGtesting.com
Printed in the USA
BVHW021020270622
640730BV00010B/115